D1608855

FEMALE FIRSTS IN THEIR FIELDS

Air & Space

Broadcasting & Journalism

Business & Industry

Entertainment & Performing Arts

Government & Politics

Literature

Science & Medicine

Sports & Athletics

FEMALE FIRSTS IN THEIR FIELDS

BUSINESS & INDUSTRY

Norma Jean Lutz

Introduction by
Roslyn Rosen

CHELSEA HOUSE PUBLISHERS
Philadelphia

To my sister, Carolyn. Without a doubt,
a female "first" in her field.

Produced by P. M. Gordon Associates, Inc.
Philadelphia, Pennsylvania

Editor in Chief Stephen Reginald
Managing Editor James D. Gallagher
Production Manager Pamela Loos
Art Director Sara Davis
Director of Photography Judy L. Hasday
Senior Production Editor Lisa Chippendale
Publishing Coordinator James McAvoy

Picture research by Artemis Picture Research Group, Inc.
Cover illustration by Cliff Spohn
Cover design by Keith Trego

Frontispiece: Oprah Winfrey

The Chelsea House World Wide Web site address is
http://www.chelseahouse.com

First Printing

1 3 5 7 9 8 6 4 2

Library of Congress Cataloging-in-Publication Data

Lutz, Norma Jean.
    Female firsts in their fields. Business & industry / Norma Jean Lutz.
        p. cm.
    Includes bibliographical references and index.
    Summary: Discusses the lives and business careers of six women:
Madam C. J. Walker, Katharine Graham, Mary Kay Ash, Martha
Stewart, Oprah Winfrey, and Sherry Lansing.
    ISBN 0-7910-5142-0 (hardcover)
    1. Women executives–United States–Case studies–Juvenile
Literature. 2. Businesswomen–United States–Case studies–
Juvenile literature. 3. Women in professions–United States–Case
Studies–Juvenile literature. [1. Businesswomen. 2. Women–Biography.]
I.Title. II. Title: Business & industry. III. Title: Business and industry.
HD6054.4.U6L87   1998
658.4′09′0820973–dc21   98-40821
                                                                            CIP
                                                                            AC

CONTENTS

INTRODUCTION

Roslyn Rosen

Whether I was a toddler, it struck me that the other people in my family's New York apartment building were different. They did not use their hands when they talked, and they did not have to watch each other speak. I had been born deaf, and I felt sorry for them because they did not know the joy of drawing pictures in the air. They could not splash ideas into the air with a jab of the finger or a wave of the hand. Not until later did I realize the downside of being deaf–I couldn't communicate directly with my grandparents and extended family members, I depended on others to make important phone calls for me, and I found life's opportunities narrower, in part because I had few deaf (let alone female) role models.

Gallaudet University in Washington, D.C., is the only college for deaf students in the world. I arrived there in September 1958. It was a haven where sign language was part of the educational process, where there were deaf professors, and where opportunities for extracurricular leadership abounded. At Gallaudet I met deaf female professionals for the first time, although there were probably not more than three or four. The president and administrators of Gallaudet were all males who could hear–typical of school administrations during those years.

In my first month at Gallaudet, I also met the man who would become my husband. My destiny was charted: major in something that I could use as a homemaker (since that would be my job), get married, have a bunch of kids, and live happily ever after. This was the expectation for women in the late 1950s and early 1960s. And I stuck to the script: I majored in art with an emphasis on education and English, got married, and had three children. My life was complete–or so I thought.

The 1960s were turbulent and thought-provoking years. The civil rights movement and the beginnings of a women's movement emphasized human rights and equality for all. I came to see how alike the issues were that faced women, people of color, and people with disabilities, in terms of human rights and respect for human differences. Multicultural studies are vital for this understanding. Changes were occurring at an accelerating rate. Those changes affected my husband and me by broadening our traditional gender roles. With my husband's support, I pursued a master's degree in education of deaf students and later a doctoral degree in education administration. From my first job as a part-time sign language teacher, I eventually joined the faculty at Gallaudet University. In 1981 I was promoted to dean of the College for Continuing Education, and in 1993, to vice president for academic affairs.

During the formative years of my career, many of my role models and mentors were deaf men who had reached positions of leadership. They hired, taught, advised, and encouraged me. There were times when I felt the effects of the "glass ceiling" (an invisible barrier that keeps women or minorities from rising any higher). Sometimes I needed to depend on my male colleagues because my access to "old boy" networks or decision makers was limited. When I became involved with the National Association of the Deaf (NAD), the world's oldest organization of deaf people, I met deaf women who became role models–Dr. Gertie Galloway was the first deaf female president of the NAD, and Marcella Meyer had founded the Greater Los Angeles Community Service of the Deaf (GLAD). In 1980 I was elected to the board of directors of the National Association of the Deaf, and in 1990, I became the second woman elected president of NAD.

When I became a dean at Gallaudet in 1981, I also became a member of the school's Council of Deans, which at the time included only two deaf deans and two female deans. I was the only deaf woman dean. The vice president was a white male, and he once commented that top administrators often build management teams in their own image. I have found that to be true. As a dean, I was the highest-ranking deaf woman at Gallaudet, and I was able to hire and help a number of young deaf female professionals within the College for Continuing Education and our regional centers around the country. In the five years that I have been vice president at Gallaudet I have added many deaf, female, and minority members to my own management team. When I was the president of NAD, I hired its first deaf female executive director, Nancy Bloch. I also encouraged two of my friends, Mabs Holcomb and Sharon Wood, to write the first deaf women history book, a source of inspiration for young deaf girls.

It is important for women who have reached the top levels of their fields to advise and help younger women to become successful. It is also important for young girls to know about the ground-breaking contributions of women who came before them. The women profiled in this series of biographies overcame many obstacles to succeed. Some had physical handicaps, others fought generations of discriminatory attitudes toward women in the workplace. The world may never provide equal opportunities for every human being, but we can all work together to improve life for the next generation.

DR. ROSLYN ROSEN is the Vice President for Academic Affairs at Gallaudet University in Washington, D.C. Dr. Rosen has served as a board member and President of the National Association of the Deaf (NAD), the oldest consumer organization in the world, and was a member of the National Captioning Institute's executive board for nine years. She is currently a board member of the World Federation of the Deaf. Dr. Rosen also wears the hats of daughter, wife, mother, and proud grandmother.

MADAM C. J. WALKER

O n December 23, 1867, in a one-room dirt-floor cabin, a baby girl was born. Sarah, Owen and Minerva Breedlove's "Christmas" baby, was special. She was the first of the three Breedlove children to be born free.

Before the Civil War, Owen and Minerva were slaves on the Burney family's Grand View Plantation in Delta, Louisiana. The war ended two years before Sarah's birth, and slaves were now free. Unsure of what to do, most former slaves stayed on the plantations and became sharecroppers. They farmed the land, then shared the crops with the owners. No matter how hard they worked, at the end of each season the sharecroppers owed the owners more money than they had made.

The Breedlove children slept on the dirt floor, and Sarah remembered receiving enough coarse material for one dress a year. Before she was five, Sarah was carrying water to the workers in the cotton fields and helping with the planting.

Born to former slaves, Sarah Breedlove, who later took the name Madam C. J. Walker, became the first female self-made millionaire.

In the mornings before going to the fields, she and her mother and her older sister, Louvenia, prepared breakfast. In the evenings Sarah hoed the garden and fed the chickens. Hard work left no time for school.

On Saturdays Sarah, Louvenia, and their mother washed clothes. Using large wooden tubs on the river bank, they did laundry for themselves and for white people. The wet sheets and tablecloths were heavy, which made the work as strenuous as picking cotton.

When Sarah was seven, yellow fever broke out in Delta. Sarah's mother and father died from this disease. Her older brother, Alex, moved to Vicksburg, Mississippi, to look for work. Sarah and Louvenia were alone.

The sisters worked in the cotton fields, but the crops failed year after year. Alex moved out West, and Sarah and her sister moved across the river to Vicksburg, where they again took in laundry to make a living. After Louvenia married, Sarah lived with her sister and brother-in-law, but the brother-in-law's cruelty made her want to escape.

When she was 14, Sarah married Moses McWilliams. On June 6, 1885, she had a baby, a girl she named Lelia. Two years later, Moses died. Now Sarah was 20, a widow with a child to care for. She wondered how she would ever support herself and Lelia. Friends told her about jobs for washerwomen in St. Louis, Missouri. Wages were higher, they said, and there were no white nightriders to threaten harm to black folks.

Sarah saved money for a boat ticket and in 1888 moved to St. Louis, where she built up a good laundry business. Determined that Lelia would have a proper education, Sarah used her earnings to send her daughter to school. Yet bending over a washboard was back-breaking work. Sarah worried over what would become of them when her back wore out.

As the years passed, Sarah absorbed information and knowledge from the world around her. She observed the mannerisms and fashions of the educated black women in her church. She saw the lovely homes of the clients where she dropped off laundry. Then in 1904, she heard Margaret Murray Washington speak at a meeting of the National Association of Colored Women. This woman, wife of well-known black leader Booker T. Washington, was stately, confident, and well dressed. Her inspiring speech and fine appearance lit a fire in Sarah. She became determined to improve herself and her life.

While Sarah prided herself on her starched and ironed dresses, she agonized over her hair. It was thin and patchy. This scalp ailment, resulting from stress and poor diet, was common in her day. No remedies helped. The problem drove her to begin mixing her own pomades. After praying to discover a workable remedy, she claimed God answered her through a dream. In the dream a black man appeared and told her what to mix up and apply to her hair. Some of the remedy was only available in Africa, but she sent for it right away.

Later she said, "I put it on my scalp, and in a few weeks my hair was coming in faster than it had ever fallen out."

Since Lelia was now away at college, Sarah moved to Denver, Colorado, to be near her brother's family. Alex had died a few years earlier. In January 1906, she married Charles Joseph Walker. Taking her husband's name, Sarah adopted the title of Madam C. J. Walker.

Working days as a laundress, Sarah Walker sold her hair products door to door in the evenings. Often she gave free treatments consisting of a wash with her Vegetable Shampoo followed by an application of her Wonderful Hair Grower. The Glossine was then applied and pressed in with a heated metal comb. Black women were pleased to have hair products designed especially for them. Soon Sarah had so much business she was forced to hire other women to sell along with her.

Sarah Walker set out across the country selling tins of Glossine and Wonderful Hair Grower and signing up hundreds of agents to work for her. Meanwhile, her husband, C.J., sold eye-catching magazine and newspaper advertisements that featured photographs of Madam Walker. These ads gave customers a personal connection to Walker and convinced them that they too could have attractive hair.

As the business grew, C.J. and Sarah had differences of opinions. "When I started in business . . . with my husband," she said, "I had business disagreements with him, for when he began to make $10 a week, he thought that amount was enough and that I should be satisfied."

Female workers then earned around $10 a week, and in the South, as little as $2 a week. To Madam Walker, however, $10 a week was just the beginning. Soon she was making $35 a week in sales, which was ten times what the average female black worker was earning.

Upon her college graduation, Lelia joined her mother in Colorado. Standing straight and tall at nearly six feet, the beautiful Lelia posed as a model, adding glamour to the advertisements. Lelia had a good business mind, and she worked at filling orders and keeping records.

Sarah Walker's extensive travels convinced her that she needed a school to train her agents, whom she referred to as "hair culturists." In the summer

An advertisement for Walker's products, printed between 1917 and 1919.

of 1908, she and Lelia opened Lelia College in Pittsburgh, Pennsylvania. From the day it opened, the school never lacked for students. The graduates not only had good jobs waiting for them, they also felt they looked better—both of which inspired self-confidence.

As her income increased, Madam Walker took time to acquire the education she'd always dreamed of. She studied penmanship, letter writing, art, and music. She began to read extensively.

Leaving Lelia in charge of the Pittsburgh school, Sarah Walker moved the business to Indianapolis,

Walker shows no hesitation in taking the wheel. All her life, she encouraged women not only to seize opportunities, but to create them.

Indiana, in 1910. There she built a large factory and hired two able men to manage the company. A woman named Alice Kelly became her secretary and companion. Miss Kelly and Lelia were the only other people in the world who knew the secret formula for Madam Walker's products.

Walker invested her profits back into the business to build it up. By 1914, her gross income from company earnings was over a million dollars. Madam Walker became the first female self-made millionaire—white or black.

In 1911, Lelia married and changed her first name to A'Lelia, becoming A'Lelia Walker Robinson. She soon divorced, then adopted Mae Bryant, a little girl who worked at the Walker factory. Like her adoptive mother, Mae became a model for the company ads. She also made business trips with her grandmother, Madam Walker. That same year, Sarah and C.J. agreed to end their marriage, but Sarah used the name of Madam C. J. Walker until her death.

A'Lelia became fascinated with the Harlem area of New York City, which was alive with black politics, music, theater, and business. Eventually, A'Lelia convinced her mother to move to Harlem, where they opened yet another Lelia College.

Leaving Alice Kelly and the managers in charge of the factory, Madam Walker moved to New York City in 1916. Although she was in poor health after a lifetime of hard work, she never slowed down. She continued traveling around the country giving speeches and opening new beauty shops.

One of her last trips took her to Delta, Louisiana, where she visited the tiny one-room cabin where she was born. Who would have imagined that a child born in such poverty could achieve such phenomenal success? At one point Booker T. Washington, whose wife Walker had admired years earlier, called Sarah Walker "one of the most progressive and successful businesswomen of our race."

Late in 1916, Madam Walker purchased land in Irvington-on-Hudson near New York City and built a mansion there. She named the home Lewaro Villa in honor of her daughter, combining the first two letters from each of Lelia's names: Lelia Walker Robinson. Neighbors who at first protested a black person living in their midst came to love and respect Madam C. J. Walker.

Madam Walker used her name, her presence, and her money to promote social causes in which she believed. She gave thousands of dollars to dozens of black organizations. She encouraged women to pursue economic independence and then gave them a way to achieve it. Through the years, her company employed thousands of agents, enabling black men and women to own their own businesses, purchase homes, and educate their children.

"Don't sit down and wait for the opportunities to come," she told them. "Get up and make them!"

Sarah Breedlove Walker died on May 25, 1919, at age 51. Her last words were, "I want to live to help my race."

Tributes poured in from around the country from blacks and whites alike. They all recognized that this woman, through determination, imagination, and hard work, had made an amazing contribution to the world in which she lived.

KATHARINE GRAHAM

By the time Katharine "Kay" Meyer was born in 1917, her father, Eugene Meyer, was already a Wall Street multimillionaire. Shortages of dye and copper during World War I led Eugene Meyer to found companies in these fields, adding millions to his net worth. His corporations, Allied Chemical and Dye Corporation and Anaconda Copper, were crucial to the United States during the war.

As a child, Kay wasn't aware of the vast family fortune. She was born fourth in a family of five children and spent her early years with nannies and governesses in New York City while her parents were busy with various projects in Washington, D.C. The children did not move to Washington until Katharine was four years old.

The Washington home, called Crescent Place, was an opulent mansion with columns in front, a circle drive, and decorative fountains. The family alternated between Crescent Place and their home in New York, the rural Mount Kisco estate where they had vegetable gardens and grazing cattle.

Kay lived in the shadow of her older siblings and her

Katharine Meyer Graham in her office at the Washington Post *in 1964.*

Katharine Meyer (second from right) joins other Vassar students to promote the American Youth Congress of 1936.

imposing and famous parents, who were neither warm nor affectionate. Alongside the other family members, she has said, she felt like a "plodding peasant."

Following in the steps of her older sisters, Kay attended the elite Madeira preparatory school for girls. During her junior year her father purchased a struggling newspaper, the *Washington Post*, for $825,000. Kay knew nothing of the transaction until she came home for the summer. From her first visit to the paper in June 1933, the paper "was constantly part of my life," she said. "My family owned it, cared deeply about it, and was immersed in the minutiae of its daily travails." That summer she worked as a copy girl in the *Post*'s women's department.

In the fall of 1934, Kay went to Vassar College in New York state. On campus, she was an outspoken leader, active in the Student Strike Against War. Because of increasing conflicts in Europe and Russia, the students wanted to make it clear they were against involvement in another world war. As a spokesperson for Vassar, Kay was featured on a CBS radio program.

From Vassar, Kay moved to Chicago, where she did graduate work at the University of Chicago. Here she met people of backgrounds different from her own and found herself enjoying intellectual discussions and debates.

Following graduation from the university, through her father's connections with friends and family in California, Kay became a reporter with the *San Francisco News*. She learned how to write to tight deadlines and came to understand the inner workings of a newspaper office. Most of her reporter buddies, who were all men, had no idea she was the daughter of the East Coast millionaire who owned the *Post*.

In the spring of 1939, Kay's father came to California and during his visit reminded her he wanted her to come back to Washington and work for *his* paper. Within a year of her move back home, she met and married Philip Graham. Graham was an ambitious young man from a dairy farm in Florida, who had managed to get into Harvard Law School with some political pull. When Kay met him, he was serving as clerk to a Supreme Court judge.

Shortly after they were married, the United States entered World War II.

Because of her wealth, Kay could afford to move from city to city, following Phil as he moved from camp to camp. When her husband was sent overseas, Kay returned to Washington and the *Post*, at

In 1962 Katharine Graham examines an issue of ART- news *with her husband, Phil, who has just purchased control of the magazine.*

one point fielding calls from angry subscribers in the paper's complaint department.

Before the war's end, Eugene Meyer was talking to Phil about taking over ownership of the *Post*. It wasn't an easy decision for Phil Graham, whose own father wanted him to return to Florida. When he at last agreed to work for the *Post*, he started as Meyer's right-hand man and quickly learned the ins and outs of the newspaper.

While Phil was building a corporate empire and transforming the *Post* into a recognized and highly respected newspaper, Kay Graham turned to home-making and rearing their four children—three boys and a girl. She knew little about running a household and had to learn things from the ground up. Although she hired a nanny and a cook, they did have days off, and during those times Kay felt the most unprepared.

When her son Donny was a baby, for instance, Kay put rubber nipples in a pot to boil to disinfect them, then went to another room to make phone calls for a party. The smell of something burning sent her racing to the kitchen, where flames leapt from the glass pot. She grabbed it, put it in the sink, turned on the cold water–and the pot exploded. "I couldn't help wondering how the children would fare if I took care of them all the time," she said.

With regard to money matters, even though Kay was worth millions, she confessed she didn't know the difference between income and capital and had no idea what a mortgage was. Her parents had never discussed money matters with their children.

In later years, Phil Graham was diagnosed as manic-depressive. His moods often swung violently, from deep depression to exuberance. His behavior became irrational. These were agonizing years for the Graham family, as they sought medical help and consultation. Phil, however, grew worse. Through it all, Kay was determined to hold her family together.

In the summer of 1963, Phil seemed better, but on a medical leave from the hospital, he shot himself to death on August 3. In a matter of moments, Kay Graham went from homemaker to decision maker. What was to become of the *Washington Post*?

The day before Phil's funeral, Katharine Graham addressed the *Post*'s board of directors and assured them that the paper would go on and that she would not sell it. In the midst of deep grief, yet determined to save the *Post*, Katharine set about to learn the business. She was surprised to discover that she loved her job and that she loved the newspaper.

BUSINESS & INDUSTRY

Graham and the Washington Post's *executive editor, Ben Bradlee, smile after winning one of the court decisions that led to publication of the "Pentagon Papers" in 1971.*

Later, her daughter, Elizabeth (called Lally), would say about her mother, "It was a tremendous transition to go from being an excellent mother to being an excellent tycoon." But Katharine Graham did just that.

Although she was shy, insecure, and terrified, she grew into the role of an executive heading a company that by this time owned other newspapers and a television station. Through on-the-job training, Katharine, at 46, had to learn to trust her own abilities and to run the paper as she saw fit rather than copy the methods of her late husband. "I had very little idea of what I was supposed to be doing," she said, "so I set out to learn."

She found the strength she needed, and soon she was making changes that improved the business. She wanted the *Post* to be the best paper in the country, and she made it the best by spending large amounts of money to hire the best writers and editors.

In June 1971 the *Post* and Katharine Graham themselves became headline news. That was the year the "Pentagon Papers" were published in the *Post* after a federal judge had halted their publication in the *New York Times*. The "Pentagon Papers" were a top-secret detailed history of the Vietnam War decision-making process, and it was Graham who made the decision to defy the government, risking steep fines and a possible prison sentence. Later, however, the Supreme Court ruled in her favor.

Later, because Katharine Graham encouraged

investigative journalism, two *Post* reporters, Bob Woodward and Carl Bernstein, discovered information that uncovered the Watergate scandal. The *Post* was out in front of every other paper, breaking news on the cover-ups and payoffs that tracked the affair all the way to the White House. Threats came from the executive branch of the government that the licenses for the two *Post* television stations would not be renewed. In spite of the threats, the paper continued to publish Woodward and Bernstein's stories. The Watergate scandal finally caused Richard Nixon to step down as president in August 1974.

In 1991, a month before her 74th birthday, Graham turns over to her son Donald (left) the position of chief executive officer at the Post. *Ben Bradlee looks on.*

Although Graham has been called courageous for her decisions during that time, she says, "The truth is that I never felt there was much choice . . . Once I found myself in the deepest water in the middle of the current, there was no going back."

A union strike in October 1975 was particularly devastating for Katharine Graham. Before the strike, pressmen disabled 70 presses, started a fire, and assaulted the pressroom foreman. As the strike dragged on for weeks, Graham was able to hire nonunion workers, call on volunteer help, repair the presses, and keep the *Post* in circulation. Several unions were involved, and slanderous language and hard feelings increased as the strike stretched into March 1976. Graham said, when the strike negotiations were finally over, "in the end we had stayed on the tightrope and reached the other side."

The eldest Graham son, Donald, became publisher of the *Post* in 1979, at which time Katharine became chair of the board of directors and stayed on as the paper's chief executive officer.

Because she wanted to tell her own story, and the stories of her parents and her husband, Phil, Katharine began working on her memoirs. Her book, *Personal History*, took six and a half years to research and write. She conducted 250 interviews with classmates, family members, and associates, and she wrote 625 pages in longhand on yellow legal pads. The book later won a Pulitzer Prize in the biography category and became a best-seller.

Although she came into the top job at the *Washington Post* unprepared, Katharine Meyer Graham turned out to be a better business manager than either her father or her husband. And she became one of the most influential women in the United States.

After all these years, Katharine Graham admits

she's never lost her love of newspapers. "Every day is compelling," she says. "I love news—if somebody writes a great story, it excites me still."

And to this day, she still calls up the *Post* to suggest a good news story!

MARY KAY ASH

"Honey, you can do it."

As a little girl, Mary Kay Wagner heard these words from her mother hundreds of times. They were words Mary Kay took to heart and applied to all areas of her life.

She was born in the small town of Hot Wells, Texas, sometime around the outbreak of World War I, about 1914. (Mary Kay refuses to tell her exact age.) Her parents owned and operated a hotel; unfortunately, her father came down with tuberculosis and spent three years in a sanitarium. Although Edward Wagner returned home, he was unable to work for the rest of his life.

The family sold the hotel and moved to Houston, where Mary Kay's mother leased a cafe near the railroad depot and worked long hours cooking good meals for the railroad workers. It fell to Mary Kay, whose older brothers and sisters were grown and gone, to keep house and care for her father.

If she didn't know how to prepare a dish, she called her mother at the cafe and asked. Her mother would take the time to give her instructions and always ended by saying,

Mary Kay Ash receives a Horatio Alger Award in 1978 for her business success.

BUSINESS & INDUSTRY

Even as a child in Houston, Mary Kay was determined to succeed.

"Honey, you can do it." Mary Kay later commented, "Her words became the theme of my childhood. They have stayed with me all of my life."

In school, Mary Kay was very competitive. She worked to become the best typist in her class and entered debate competitions and speech contests. She completed high school in three years rather than the customary four, and she earned straight A's.

At 18, she married Ben Rogers, a local musician. The couple had three children. Following a stint in the army during World War II, Ben deserted his family, leaving Mary Kay to support the children alone. It was one of the lowest points in her life.

While working as a church secretary, Mary Kay sold Stanley products part-time. Selling was something she enjoyed, and soon she was selling Stanley products full-time. As she realized she needed to learn more about sales, she borrowed $12 to travel to Dallas for a sales convention. At the convention, one of the sales representatives was crowned "Queen of Sales" and won an alligator purse. Mary Kay determined that the next year she would be the queen. And she was. However, she was disappointed when that year's prize turned out to be an underwater flashlight called a "flounder light," used for fishing!

At that moment she vowed if she were ever in a position to do so, she would give prizes to employees that would inspire them, not disappoint them.

In 1953, Mary Kay was offered a job with World Gift. She took over the Houston operation and was soon named area manager. From there she was promoted to national training director. This meant that she had to travel extensively as she helped build up the business in 43 states. But no matter how hard she worked, she was continually passed over for promotions, which went only to male employees. Her salary was half that of her male counterparts.

During sales meetings her supervisors often dismissed her ideas and accused her of "thinking just like a woman." How she longed for a time when thinking like a woman would become an asset rather than a liability!

By 1963, Mary Kay had remarried and was earning around $25,000 a year with Gift World. The company then demoted her from the position of national training director and offered her a less important position as unit manager. She turned it down and retired.

After a few weeks of "retirement," she became restless. Thinking back on her 25-plus years in business, she considered writing a book outlining her vision of how a company should be run. She called it her "dream company." The basic premise would be the Golden Rule: "Do unto others as you would have them do unto you," based on the Bible scripture Matthew 7:12. Quickly she realized she didn't want just to write about it—she wanted to start an actual company based on these principles. Casting about for the perfect product, she chose the skin-care products she'd been using for a number of years.

Years earlier, while still a Stanley salesperson, Mary Kay had visited the home of a woman who was experimenting with skin-care products derived from her father's tanning solutions. Mary Kay was so impressed, she took home a shoebox-full that very day. In 1961, she had purchased the formula to ensure that she would have a continuing supply. These cosmetics became the products for her new business.

She then hired a manufacturer to make the products and planned to open a small shop in Dallas. A month before the planned opening, her husband died of a heart attack. Mary Kay was alone again. Her attorney and her accountant advised her to sell before she lost everything. But Mary Kay, who is a Christian, believed that "when God closes a door, He always opens a window."

Her son, 20-year-old Richard, agreed to become her financial administrator and business partner. They opened on schedule—September 13, 1963. Called "Beauty by Mary Kay" (later Mary Kay Cosmetics, Inc.), the company started with nine salespeople—friends of Mary Kay. After one year in business they had sold $198,000 worth of skin-care products!

Mary Kay designed her company to conduct small "classes" in the privacy of clients' homes. There the women would be taught the fine points of skin care. She called her salespeople "beauty consultants."

After the first year, the company held a convention and called it, simply, "Seminar." Years later Seminar would be a gala event of gigantic proportions. The first one, however, convened in a warehouse, where boned chicken and Jell-O salad were served on paper plates. Two hundred consultants attended. With great optimism, Mary Kay predicted there would be 3,000 at the second seminar. She was mistaken. By 1965, the number had grown to 11,000!

Each consultant worked as an independent agent and was free to build her business as large as she wanted. Unlike other sales companies, Mary Kay assigned no territories. A consultant vacationing in Hawaii could recruit a new consultant there. That new consultant would be under a director in her home area. Mary Kay calls this the "adoptee" program.

Business experts said this could never work. But it has worked and continues to work. Mary Kay calls it the "Go-Give" principle, based on giving, not just getting. "Everyone helps everyone else," she says. Because of this system and the relationships among the women consultants, the company has been called a "vast sorority."

In 1969 Mary Kay presented the first of the famous pink Cadillacs to the top five independent sales directors. In later years, General Motors, the auto maker that manufactures the prize cars, would create an official color and dub it "Mary Kay pink." Remembering the underwater flashlight incident, Mary Kay has used mink coats, diamonds, and new cars as gifts to motivate her salespeople.

In the early 1970s, the plant in Dallas was ex-

A collection of the kinds of products that have made Mary Kay famous.

panded, as new distribution and training centers were set up. That same year, the company expanded into Canada and Australia. The firm moved into new corporate headquarters in 1977, a gleaming structure of bronzed-gold glass and beige brick—which was paid for in cash when it opened.

Mary Kay remained at the head of the company, serving as an encourager and business manager. She trained her consultants to prioritize their lives, putting God first, family second, and career third. Her greatest goal was never to make money but rather to provide women with an unlimited opportunity for personal and financial success. It's been said her company sells dreams as well as makeup.

From the outset, the firm's symbol has been the bumblebee. It's been proven that, aerodynamically speaking, the bumblebee's wings are too small to carry its large body in flight, but the bumblebee doesn't know that, so it flies anyway. Mary Kay likes to think "our Divine Creator whispered, 'You can do it!' so it did!"

In the same way, the women who come into the company aren't always aware at first that they can succeed. But "with help and encouragement," says Mary Kay, "they find their wings—and then they fly very well indeed." Some of her top performers are awarded diamond-studded bumblebee pins.

Her book, *Mary Kay on People Management*, was adopted for use in classes at a dozen universities, including Harvard. Published in 1984, the book remained on the *New York Times* best-seller list for 11 weeks. This success suggests that the business world is listening to Mary Kay, the first woman to chair a Fortune 500 company.

Mary Kay, Inc. has grown from a small direct-sales company to the largest direct seller of skincare products in the United States. The 500,000 independent beauty consultants live all around the world.

In her autobiography, *Mary Kay: The Success Story of America's Most Dynamic Businesswoman*, Mary Kay writes, "It took a long time for God to get me ready for the job He had for me. All my years of experience, trial and error, hard work, and disappointment were necessary before I could be guided to form this company."

Now in her eighties, Mary Kay continues to work at the office headquarters, overseeing the support staff and personally answering upwards of 7,000 letters monthly.

Before leaving home each morning she fastens her own diamond-studded bumblebee pin on her right shoulder. The pin serves as a perpetual reminder of her mother's words: "Honey, you can do it."

Her mother was right!

MARTHA STEWART

On a typical day, Martha Stewart rises before dawn. By noon she will have completed her 5:30 A.M. workout, read the papers, written memos to her top staff, appeared on a morning news program, held a meeting about a new line of Martha Stewart towels, and visited the offices of Martha Stewart Living Omnimedia, where she talked with some of the 150 people who work on her magazine, *Martha Stewart Living*.

A person who needs very little sleep and who possesses seemingly endless drive and energy, Stewart puts in 20-hour workdays to keep her chain of enterprises in the national spotlight. She gardens, she cooks, she decorates, she remodels, she even raises chickens–then she writes about what she does. Or makes a video. Or describes it on a national television special. It's been said that "Martha Stewart has had more influence on how Americans eat, entertain, and decorate their homes and gardens, than any one person in our history."

Martha learned about gardening from her father in the backyard of their small home in Nutley, New Jersey. Born

Since childhood, Martha Stewart has been a talented gardener.

37

in 1941 to Polish parents, she was the second of six children. Her father, Edward Kostyra, was a pharmaceuticals salesman. He failed to achieve his high goals in life, but he expected his children to excel in all that they did. Kostyra's widow (also named Martha) said in later years that her husband was a perfectionist and highly competitive. "He wouldn't plant six tomato plants–he'd plant 80," she said. "And he would compete with a neighbor to see who could grow the longest beans."

About her father, Stewart said, "My father took me under his wing, and I learned everything. He taught me how to garden, how to use all his tools. He helped me with public speaking . . . He taught by 'I'll beat it into you.'" She was quick to add that she didn't mind, because she appreciated tough teaching.

Of all the Kostyra children, Martha was the natural gardener. She enjoyed weeding and cultivating in the hot sun. From childhood, she was also entranced by food and cooking and often helped her mother prepare meals. While she was still in grammar school, Stewart organized birthday parties for neighborhood children. In high school, she prepared a breakfast for the school football team. Sewing too was part of Martha's home life. She and her mother made her first formal dress out of ice-satin peau de soie with underskirts of pink silk net.

As the eldest daughter, Martha was responsible for much of the care of her brothers and sisters. She was in high school when the youngest, Laura, was born. In a house with one bathroom and shared bedrooms, Martha dreamed of having frilly curtains and privacy. During this time, she became an incurable insomniac, staying up until all hours of the night, a condition that followed her into adulthood.

Because their middle-class family had no money

Already a model, the teenage Martha (center) serves as "queen of the hop" at a high school ball, wearing a gown she helped to make.

for college, Martha knew she had to win academic scholarships. To make it happen, in high school she served on a number of committees and was a member of half a dozen or more clubs. While other college-bound students took two years of math, Martha enrolled in four. Her first writing and editing experience came as she wrote for the high school literary quarterly, *The Gauntlet*.

On top of this demanding schedule, she took bus trips into New York City to attempt to break into the modeling business. Her father encouraged her by taking photos of her, teaching her how to pose and become comfortable in front of the camera. Her break came during her senior year when she was chosen to appear in a Lifebuoy soap commercial. The spot aired on a Saturday night during one of the more popular shows of that era, *Have Gun, Will Travel*.

Martha turned down a full scholarship from New York University, preferring a partial scholarship to Barnard College. Modeling jobs—now with Tarryton cigarettes and Breck shampoo—supplemented her scholarship. Stewart's pace at college was even more grueling than in high school, as she rose before dawn to catch the bus into New York. At Times Square she boarded the subway bound for the campus at Broadway and 116th Street. In between classes, she squeezed in modeling jobs.

In the spring of 1960, Martha met Diane Stewart Love, who insisted that Martha meet her brother, Andrew. Andrew Stewart was a student at Yale Law School. Andy and Martha fell in love and were married the next year. Martha dropped out of school for a year to support Andy during his last year of law school. She graduated the next year, 1964.

A daughter, Alexis, was born to the Stewarts in 1967. At this time, Martha quit modeling and turned to her father-in-law's profession, stockbrokerage, which appealed to her more. As a stockbroker, Martha became quite successful, earning $135,000 a year. But during the 1973 recession, she became a "nervous wreck," as she told friends later. The job lost all its appeal. "I liked the sales part of it, the human contact," she explained. "But I wanted to sell things that were fun to sell. And stocks weren't, anymore."

In the early '70s, there was a "back to the land" movement going on around the country. The Stewarts moved to Westport, Connecticut, where they purchased an 1805 Federal-style farmhouse and began to restore it. As Martha put it, they "removed the unsightly and replaced it with the beautiful." They called the farm, where Martha still lives, "Turkey Hill" for its original address—48 South Turkey Hill Road.

Martha hand-stenciled floors, painted murals, and built stone walls. Andy put up a chicken house for her fancy roosters and hens, and a Shaker-style barn that Martha designed. Together they planted orchards and gardens, maintained beehives, and eventually built a smokehouse.

It was in this setting that Martha, in 1976, started her catering business out of the basement of the old farmhouse. After the first job—a 200-guest wedding—Martha Stewart knew she was hooked. Within the decade, the catering enterprise mushroomed into a $1 million business, with clients that included prestigious corporations and celebrities. Many of the herbs and other ingredients for the catered food came right out of the Stewarts' garden. While conducting her catering business, Martha wrote articles for the *New York Times* and became a columnist for the magazine *House Beautiful*.

Meanwhile, Andy had tired of the law profession and had become fascinated with the world of publishing. In 1976, he was named executive vice president of Harry N. Abrams, Inc., a publisher of lavish "coffee-table books."

Andy's contact with publishers allowed Martha to cater a party where she met Alan Mirken, president of Crown Publishing Group. That meeting led to the publication of her first book, *Entertaining*. The book, co-written by Elizabeth Hawes, appeared just when cookbooks were becoming popular. The first run of 25,000 quickly sold out. This was the beginning of a series of colorful books, such as *Martha Stewart's Quick Cook Menus*, *Martha Stewart's Hors d'Oeuvres*, and *Martha Stewart's Pies and Tarts*. She has now written more than 14 of these books, which led to videotapes, television specials, lectures, and seminars, securing Martha's popularity and keeping her in the public eye.

In 1997 Stewart, who calls herself "an eclectic knowledge-gathering person," helps promote funding for the arts with Earle Mack, chairman of the New York State Council on the Arts.

Next came an offer from K-Mart for Martha to become their lifestyle consultant. Through K-Mart, she was able to promote her own line of bed and bath products.

In spite of traveling for about 150 days a year, Stewart still loves to garden and cook at home and doesn't mind getting her hands dirty. She may be found in the yard at her new home on Long Island, planting bare-root roses. In a 1996 interview with *McCall's* magazine, she told of having rid all her chickens of lice the day before.

In 1990 Martha launched a bimonthly magazine, *Martha Stewart Living*, which is now read by more than 1.3 million people. The magazine is published by Time Publishing Ventures, Inc., a division of Time Inc., the publishers of *Time*, *People*, and other magazines.

As Martha's career was building, her marriage was weakening. While she was on a book tour for her publication *Martha Stewart's Weddings*, Andy moved out of the big house at Turkey Hill. The couple divorced in 1990. Although the differences between the two were bitter, in later years Martha would say, "The life that I had is over, and what has taken its place is better."

As a child, Martha dreamed of becoming a teacher, and in a way, she has made that dream come true. "My dream now, in retrospect then, was to become an eclectic knowledge-gathering person, in order to be able to learn and then to teach. And I'm still doing that, so I think I am a teacher."

Stewart's goal has always been to "make homemaking glamorous again" and "to help give women back a sense of pleasure and accomplishment in their homes." No one can argue with the positive impact she has had on the homes, and the home-makers, of America.

Janet Cawley of the *Chicago Tribune* wrote that Martha Stewart is "a phenomenon of the eighties and nineties, tapping brilliantly into the stay-at-home, nesting mentality of those no longer able to shell out big bucks for travel, entertainment, or elaborate dinners out."

"At the same time," Cawley continued, "she offers a vision: life as we all would like it to be but somehow never quite manage it ourselves."

About her work, Stewart says, "I have the ideal career, because I'm constantly writing about or photographing things that I like."

That ideal career, without a doubt, has been one of the most successful in its field.

OPRAH WINFREY

The great names of daytime television crowded Radio City Music Hall in New York City. Spotlights danced across the stage as the music blared. The event was the 1987 Emmy Awards presentation. When the award for the outstanding host of a talk show was announced, the name Oprah Winfrey sent the crowds into a cheering frenzy. Effervescent and smiling, Winfrey strode confidently to the stage to receive the golden trophy.

Though she'd had her own nationally syndicated talk show for only one short year, Oprah had become an instant success. Later that same evening, she accepted yet another Emmy—this time for the show itself. In subsequent years, many more Emmys were to come her way.

In a business controlled by males (most of them white), a black woman taking the television industry by storm was unheard of. Who was Oprah Winfrey, and where had she come from?

Oprah was born January 29, 1954, to teenage parents who were not married. In fact, her father wasn't even present

TV viewers take to Oprah Winfrey because she is not just a smooth talker—she often reveals her own feelings.

45

when she was born. The name on her birth certificate was Oprah Gail, although her first name was supposed to be "Orpah" from the book of Ruth in the Bible. Someone misspelled the name, switching the "p" and the "r," and the name stuck.

Her mother moved away, leaving Oprah with her grandmother on a farm near Kosciusko, Mississippi. Her grandmother taught Oprah religious principles and was both strict and loving. Oprah learned to read when she was two-and-a-half and made her first speech at church when she was three. Because she was so bright, she was promoted from kindergarten to first grade in midyear. These early years were some of the happiest of her childhood.

The happiness and security fled when she was sent to Milwaukee to live with her mother, Vernita Lee, who worked at cleaning houses. Her long work hours made it impossible to give Oprah the attention a young daughter needs. During this time, Oprah was sexually abused by a 19-year-old cousin and also by a family friend. In later years she would say, "You lose your childhood once you've been abused."

Through these difficult years, she hid herself in books. But she also acted out, making up stories to get her mother's attention. She stole from her mother's purse and even faked a robbery in order to get a new pair of glasses—she ransacked the house, then claimed thieves had broken in and smashed her glasses.

When her mother dragged her to a detention center, intending to leave her there, they discovered it was full. Vernita Lee sent the 14-year-old Oprah to Nashville to live with her father, Vernon, and his wife, Zelma.

Vernon Winfrey, a successful barber and member of the Nashville City Council, was a strict disciplinarian. He provided Oprah with guidance, love, and security. Before coming to dinner each evening, for instance, she was required to have added five new words to her vocabulary. He demanded she read books and present him with weekly book reports—in addition to her schoolwork. Referring to this time, she later stated, "When my father took me, it changed the course of my life. He saved me."

In high school, Oprah excelled in debate and drama. At 16 she won an Elks Club oratorical contest, which guaranteed her a full scholarship to Tennessee State University. Before graduating from high school, she was hired by WVOL, a local radio station, to read newscasts on the half hour.

During her freshman year at college, she became Miss Black Nashville *and* Miss Tennessee—quite a turnaround from being a trouble-making youngster.

As a result of her entry in the Miss Black America Pageant in 1971, she was offered a job as news coanchor with Nashville's WTVF-TV. This position made her the city's first black female newscaster. At the time, she was still living at home with her strict father. She joked, "I was the only news anchor in the country who had to be home by midnight."

But Oprah wanted to expand her horizons. She landed a news job at WJZ-TV, an ABC affiliate in Baltimore, Maryland. As the coanchor on the 6:00 P.M. news, she wasn't too successful. The problem was her tender emotions; Oprah had to fight back tears when the stories were too sad. Her colleagues nicknamed her "Sarah Bernhardt," for a famous dramatic French actress of the 1920s.

She was transferred from news to a talk show called *People Are Talking*. After the very first show, she said, "This is what I was born to do. This is like breathing." For seven years, she and her cohost, Richard Sher, tackled a wide range of topics, from

*Oprah receives her 1987
Emmy Award.*

divorce to child rearing, and from the Ku Klux Klan to Siamese twins.

In 1983, the Baltimore station manager sent an audition tape of Oprah to the manager of WLS-TV in Chicago, Dennis Swanson. Swanson was impressed by the tape and by Oprah's high ratings in Baltimore. He offered her a job as anchor on *A.M. Chicago.*

In January 1984, Oprah left Baltimore and headed for the Windy City, where she expected pickets to protest her arrival, since Chicago was famous for its racial problems. There were no pickets. Her bigger problem, however, was the dull fare being presented on the morning show. That, and the fact that Phil Donahue had reigned as talk-show "king" of Chicago for 16 seasons.

Oprah changed the show's format by introducing

Open about her weight problems, Winfrey joins fans and friends on a five-kilometer walk as part of her fitness campaign in 1995.

more controversial topics and became an instant hit. Within one month the ratings were even with Donahue's. After three months, Oprah nosed ahead. This was something no one had expected. The show was expanded from a half-hour to an hour and renamed *The Oprah Winfrey Show*. In September 1986, the newly syndicated show was seen in 192 cities, and Oprah soon became one of the highest-paid performers in show business.

Viewers loved Oprah not only because she empathized with guests and their problems, but because she revealed her own feelings and past experiences. "People recognize when you are willing to

BUSINESS & INDUSTRY

Winfrey interviews the first lady, Hillary Rodham Clinton, in January 1996.

be raw and truthful," she said in an interview, "and it's a relief to have somebody not try to be perfect." One year later, in 1987, the show *and* Oprah won their first Emmy Awards.

Quincy Jones, who was producing a movie with Steven Spielberg, saw acting potential in Oprah and asked her to audition for the movie, *The Color Purple.* She got the part and was later nominated for a Golden Globe and an Academy Award for Best Supporting Actress.

In addition to being witty and spontaneous in front of the cameras, Oprah is a level-headed businesswoman. She formed her own television production company, Harpo ("Oprah" spelled backward) Productions, then purchased three television stations and a Chicago restaurant. Harpo is housed in a huge studio that Oprah had built for it in Chicago. She is the first African-American woman to own her own television studio.

Intensely interested in national affairs, she lobbies in Washington, D.C., for stricter sentencing for convicted child abusers. She's also helped write legislation to create a national databank for sex offenders.

Her incredible wealth has enabled Oprah to take on projects that are dear to her heart. At Tennessee State, she has set up a $750,000 fund to provide 10 scholarships a year. In 1989 she donated $1 million to Morehouse College in Atlanta, Georgia, one of many contributions to that community. In a housing district in Chicago, she established a "Little Sisters" program that provides counseling and assistance to young girls.

Her generosity extends past civic organizations to her friends. One year she took the entire Harpo staff to a Caribbean island for a three-day retreat. She presented her close friend Gayle King (an anchorwoman and talk-show host from Hartford, Connecticut) with a $1 million check to purchase a house. Oprah also footed the bill for a friend's wedding. Such things happen with great regularity around Oprah.

Always open and up-front about her personal struggle with weight, she has at last moved past binges and crash diets. In the past, viewers watched her shed pounds, only to quickly gain them all back again and more. Her new regimen includes three sensible meals a day and working out twice a day. Now the pounds come off and stay off. She's become fit enough to run marathons–about 26 miles–which surprised her friends and fans alike.

In spite of incredible fame and fortune, Oprah takes her position, and her responsibility to viewers, very seriously. This sense of responsibility, she believes, is why her program has remained head and shoulders above all other talk shows.

"From the beginning, my philosophy has been that people deserve to come and to leave [my show] with their dignity." This is not the case with many talk shows, where guests are ridiculed and degraded. To

In recent years Winfrey (center) has started "Oprah's Book Club" as a segment of her TV show. Here her Book Club gathering has a pajama party at the home of author Maya Angelou (seated in chair at left).

Oprah, it is a matter of service—to herself, her viewers, and most of all to God. "The greatest responsibility I feel is to my Creator, and what I try to fulfill for myself is to honor the creation."

"The fact that I was created a Black woman in this lifetime," she adds, "everything in my life is built around honoring that. I feel a sense of reverence to that. I hold it sacred."

Oprah continually asks herself this question: "What do I owe in service for having been created a Black woman?" The answer is that she wants to use *The Oprah Winfrey Show* to "change people's lives for the better."

This amazing woman has met and overcome obstacles in her life that would have stopped most people. But Oprah has persevered and excelled. Today her show is the top-rated talk show in the history of television. It is broadcast on more than 200 stations in the United States and in 12 foreign countries.

If she has any feelings of greatness, Oprah says, it is simply because ". . . I'm doing what I'm supposed to be doing on the planet—empowering people. . . . I am so grateful for my life. I wouldn't trade my life with anyone."

SHERRY LANSING

A star-studded group gathered in front of Mann's Chinese Theatre in the warm California sunshine. On this August day in 1996, the Hollywood Walk of Fame would induct the first woman into its exclusive club of studio powerhouses— a club that included old-time moviemakers such as Samuel Goldwyn, Louis B. Mayer, Harry, Jack and Sam Warner, and Darryl and David Zanuck. Today, Sherry Lansing's marker would join theirs.

The attractive brunet, flanked by her husband, William Friedkin, and stepson, Jack, was all smiles. The former high school math teacher had traveled a long way to become the chair of Paramount Pictures. Sherry Lansing is the only woman in Hollywood who is in a position to give the go-ahead to about 20 big-budget films a year. She is the most powerful woman in the motion picture industry.

Much of Sherry's determination and drive came from observing her mother, a German Jew who escaped Nazi persecution at 17. When Margot Heimann came to America she spoke only German. She took a job selling dresses, learned

Once a math teacher, Sherry Lansing became the most powerful woman in Hollywood.

to speak fluent English, and eventually married a real estate developer, David Duhl. The couple had two children—Sherry, born in 1944, and Judy, who came along six years later.

When Sherry was nine years old, her father died of a heart attack. Her mother supported the family by collecting rent on the properties her husband had owned. When the office manager, a man, told her she wouldn't be able to do it, Sherry remembers her mother saying, "I'll do it. Teach me and I'll do it." Those simple words were to have a profound effect upon Sherry in later years.

Eventually Margot went back to being mother and homemaker when she married Norton Lansing, a successful furniture-company representative. The marriage was a good one and brought stability back into the home.

Always an overachiever, Sherry Lansing attended the University of Chicago's Laboratory High School, a school for gifted students, and graduated with honors in 1962. At Northwestern University, she minored in theater and majored in English and math. Her mother urged her to marry, and Sherry married her boyfriend, Michael Brownstein, during her sophomore year.

She graduated with high honors in 1966. "I got all A's in college," she commented later, "not because I'm so bright, but because I studied all the time."

Brownstein, a medical student, transferred to Los Angeles for an internship. Sherry taught high school math in the Watts area, one year after the riots there. Her teaching stint lasted only a few years. The passion for teaching was gone, she admitted later, and she was becoming the same kind of "repetitive" teacher that she disliked so much when she was in school.

With her long dark-brown hair, wide-set blue eyes,

and high cheekbones, Sherry has been compared to Sophia Loren and Jacqueline Onassis. Using her good looks to her advantage, she turned to modeling. She appeared in television commercials for Max Factor Company and Alberto-Culver Company in 1969 and 1970. Between assignments, she took on bit parts in the movies. "I was a terrible actress," she said in an interview a decade later. "I found it so difficult and painful to do."

In the process, however, she learned she was fascinated by movie production. She wanted to know what all the technicians on the set were doing. Consequently, she enrolled in film courses at the University of California at Los Angeles. During this time, she and Michael were divorced, and she found herself looking even more urgently for her place in life.

Not afraid of hard work or of starting at the bottom, Sherry read scripts for $5 an hour for Wagner International. Within two years, she was working with writers and developing screen plays as executive story editor.

From Wagner she advanced to executive story editor at Metro-Goldwyn-Mayer (MGM). This was the highest "nonactor" position a woman could attain at a major studio at that time. Lansing's talents and abilities, however, took her even higher.

In 1977 she was promoted to vice president of creative affairs. This position made her hungry to be even more directly involved with production. When she was offered the job of head of production at Columbia Pictures, she jumped at the chance. Her career took off as she developed two important films in 1979: *The China Syndrome* and *Kramer vs. Kramer*.

In casting *Kramer*, Lansing fought to use an unknown actress named Meryl Streep. The movie not only won an Academy Award for Best Picture,

Lansing (seated, left), actress Jane Fonda (right), and studio executive Verna Fields are honored during a luncheon at the Women in Film Crystal Awards in 1981.

but Streep also received an Oscar for Best Supporting Actress.

The next year, at age 35, Lansing was named president of production at 20th Century Fox, the first woman in Hollywood to hold such a position. Along with the job came frustrations, since there were three men higher than she was. She still lacked the power to give big pictures a green light.

After three years at Fox, she left to form her own company. Her partner was Stanley Jaffe, who had produced *Kramer vs. Kramer*. The movie that made Sherry Lansing famous was *Fatal Attraction*, the biggest movie hit of 1987. Another hit came in 1993, *Indecent Proposal*, which grossed more than $100 million in the United States alone.

These hits led to an offer from the struggling Paramount studio for the top position in the company. Lansing accepted.

In her search for pictures that "stir emotion," she came upon a script entitled *Forrest Gump*. The picture had been offered to Warner, but Warner abandoned it. Lansing bought it and produced it (with Tom Hanks as part of the package deal) at great financial risk. *Gump* went on that next year to become one of the top five money-making movies of all time. The movie won Academy Awards for Best Picture, Best Actor, and Best Director. The new head of Paramount had proven herself once and for all.

To Paramount, Sherry brought an element of stability. Within a year, the company moved from sixth place in overall market share to third place—just behind Warner and Disney. Profits shot up, the company made 20 films a year instead of only 14, and big-name talent came to Paramount and stayed. More important to Sherry, she now had the power to green-light $50 million projects!

Fifteen months into her move to Paramount, Viacom took over the company. Lansing's position, however, remained secure.

As she moved up through the ranks, Lansing received more than her share of snide accusations. Some called her "window dressing." Others referred to her promotions as "publicity ploys." In spite of these remarks, many stars were won over by her technical expertise and emotional support. Michael Douglas said he was amazed by the way she pointed out problems and then suggested solutions. Sherry Lansing, he said, was "a great sounding board . . . never afraid to voice her own opinions."

"Her enthusiasm level is astounding," one observer said. "She commanded a roomful of egos." This comment referred to grueling briefing sessions between Sherry and her colleagues where she presented plans and ideas, including budgets—a process in which some egos are bound to be bruised.

"People *like* her. They respect her," says her former partner, Stanley Jaffe. "It's not because she demands it. She earns it."

A former agent and good friend, Sue Mengers, says that Lansing's pleasant demeanor "is not an act. She is what she appears to be, amazing as it is."

Sherry has been described as shrewd but not shrill. She's never felt she had to be overly aggressive or act "tough" to make her viewpoints known. "I would like to think of myself as a strong woman. But I'm not a tough woman," she commented. "I don't understand why human decency, kindness, respect for people, have to be mutually exclusive from strength."

In spite of her level of power, Lansing prefers to stay in the shadows. In the summer of 1994, she arrived unannounced on the Irish set of Mel Gibson's epic film *Braveheart*. In spite of cold rain and

Lansing with husband William Friedkin and his son, Jack.

mud, she sat for hours under a makeshift tarp, fetched her own coffee, and quietly watched the video monitors. That's how she likes it. "It's not about power or status," she says. "It's not about money. It's about the movies and that's all I ever cared about."

In 1990, Lansing met producer/director (*The Exorcist*) William Friedkin at an Academy Awards party. "Meeting Billy was like meeting my best friend and my best lover in one person," she said. They were married three months later.

Lansing feels that women are more inclined to

define themselves by relationships than by a job or a career. "Loving somebody is important. And being loved back," she explains. She describes her life now as being more balanced, something she feels she lacked before the marriage. Since Friedkin has shared custody of his son, Jack, there is now a child in Lansing's life. "I'm so lucky [Jack] has a mother who lets him love me." Jack's mother is actress Lesley-Anne Down.

Lansing is smitten with the movies. And she prefers a movie theater to a studio screening room. She likes to stand in line, buy her popcorn, and see the picture with other people. She comments that she's seen nearly every film made in the last decade.

Behind the scenes, likewise, her excitement for the movie-making process has never diminished. "It's like an adrenaline rush when I walk onto a sound stage or a set—it's alive," she says. Then she adds, "You can see why people fall in love on movie sets. It's a magical place, and nothing else exists."

CHRONOLOGY

1884   Elizabeth Arden was born in Woodbridge, Ontario, Canada. She marketed an international line of cosmetics, operating beauty salons in Europe for the wealthy and elite.

1913   Rose Morgan was born in Shelby, Michigan. She opened Rose Meta House of Beauty, which became the largest black-owned beauty salon in the United States. A second, more chic salon, House of Beauty, made $200,000 in its first year.

1871   Helena Rubenstein was born in Kraków, Poland. She developed a line of cosmetics and operated beauty salons in Europe and the United States.

1903   Maggie Walker opened the St. Luke Penny Savings Bank and served as president, becoming the first African American to found a bank. She also started a newspaper, the *St. Luke Herald*, and served as editor.

1922   Helen Rogers Reid becomes vice president of the *New York Tribune*, which eventually became the *New York Herald Tribune*, the most powerful newspaper in the nation. Reid became president of the paper in 1947.

1927   Dorothy Arzner becomes the first female film director, after starting as a typist at Paramount. She was the first person to use film theme music and overhead microphones.

1929   Marjorie Child Husted becomes director of the Betty Crocker Homemaking Service of General Mills.

1939   Dorothy Schiff, a liberal social reformer, purchases the *New York Post* newspaper in 1939 and becomes publisher in 1942.

1955   After filling concert halls in Europe, Marian Anderson becomes the first African American to sing at the Metropolitan Opera House in New York City.

1966   Mary Georgene Wells opens her own advertising agency, Wells, Rich, Green, Inc., which by 1972 becomes the top U.S. ad agency, with Wells the highest-paid woman executive in the nation.

1967   Muriel F. Siebert becomes the first woman to own a seat on the New York Stock Exchange. Muriel Siebert and Company is a thriving brokerage business.

1976   At ABC, Barbara Walters becomes the first woman to coanchor the evening news for a major network and the first woman television journalist to command a million-dollar salary.

1977   Debi Fields opens an outlet of Mrs. Fields Cookies, which expands into more than 600 stores around the nation and overseas.

FURTHER READING

Acker, Ally. *Reel Women: Pioneers of the Cinema, 1986 to the Present.* New York: Continuum, 1991.

Ash, Mary Kay. *Mary Kay: The Success Story of America's Most Dynamic Business Woman.* New York: Harper & Row, 1987.

Bundles, A'Lelia Perry. *Madam C. J. Walker.* Philadelphia: Chelsea House, 1991.

Current Biography Yearbook 1993. Edited by Judith Graham. New York: H. W. Wilson, 1993.

David, Deborah. *Katharine the Great.* Second edition. Bethesda, Md.: A Zenith Edition, National Press, 1987.

Jeffrey, Laura S. *Collective Biographies: Great American Businesswomen.* Springfield, N.J.: Enslow, 1996.

Mansfield, Stephanie. "Hollywood's Leading Lady." *Working Woman,* April 1995: 35–39, 87–93.

Newsmakers 92: The People Behind Today's Headlines. Edited by Louise Mooney. Detroit and Washington, D.C.: Gale Research, 1992.

Price-Groff, Claire. *Extraordinary Women Journalists.* New York: Children's Press (Grolier), 1997.

Rediger, Pat. *Great African Americans in Business.* New York: Crabtree, 1996.

PHOTO CREDITS
Archive Photos/Howard Sachs: p. 2; Schomburg Center for Research in Black Culture, Division of Photographs and Prints/New York Public Library: pp. 10, 15, 16; AP/Wide World Photos: pp. 18, 24, 25, 49, 52; UPI/Corbis-Bettmann: pp. 20, 29; Newsweek/Vytas Valaitas: p. 22; Courtesy of Mary Kay, Inc.: pp. 30, 33; Randee St. Nicholas: p. 36; Courtesy of Harry Ransom Humanities Research Center, The University of Texas at Austin, p. 39; AP/Wide World Photos/Tim Roske: p. 42; AP/Wide World Photos/Steve Green: pp. 44, 50; Archive Photos/Tom Gates: p. 48; AP/Wide World Photos/Tom Keller: p. 54; AP/Wide World Photos/Rasmussen: p. 58; Archive Photos/Darleen Hammond: p. 60.

INDEX

ABOUT THE AUTHOR

Norma Jean Lutz, who lives in Tulsa, Oklahoma, has been writing professionally since 1977. She is the author of more than 250 short stories and articles as well as 28 books–fiction and nonfiction. Of all the writing she does, she most enjoys writing children's books.